calm reflections

calm reflections

inspiring lessons for a stress-free life

www.youaretheauthor.com

Published in the UK in 2003 exclusively for
WHSmith Limited
Greenbridge Road
Swindon SN3 3LD
www.WHSmith.co.uk
by Tangent Publications, an imprint of
Axis Publishing Limited

Conceived and created by
Axis Publishing Limited
8c Accommodation Road
London NW11 8ED
www.axispublishing.co.uk

Creative Director: Siân Keogh
Editorial Director: Brian Burns
Production Manager: Tim Clarke

ISBN 0–9543620–5–5

2 4 6 8 10 9 7 5 3 1

Printed and bound in China

about this book

Calm Reflections brings together an inspirational selection of powerful and life-affirming phrases that have in one way or another helped people to live less stressful lives, and combines them with evocative and gently amusing animal photographs that bring out the full humour and pathos of the human condition.

We all have too much to do and not enough time to do it in, and rush around getting ever more tired and stressed-out. These inspiring examples of wit and wisdom, written by real people based on their true-life experiences, enable us to slow down, rethink our priorities and rediscover our love of life. As two of the entries so aptly put it – enjoy the little things, and take life as it comes.

So take it easy, relax and chill out!

about the author

Why have one author when you can have the world? This book has been compiled

using the incredible resource that is the world wide web. From the many hundreds

of contributions that were sent to the website, *www.youaretheauthor.com*, we

have selected the ones that best sum up what a stress-free life is all about – making

time for the things you enjoy and finding personal fulfilment.

Please continue to send in your special

views, feelings and advice about life – you

never know, you too might see your words of

wisdom in print one day!

www.youaretheauthor.com

Keep calm.

In any situation, I perform a lot
better if I'm as calm as I can be.
Panic stops me thinking straight.

anon@youaretheauthor.com

Breathe.

When I'm getting stressed
about something, my breathing
gets shallow and makes me feel
worse. By telling myself to breathe
I can focus clearly as well as
breathe properly.

anon@youaretheauthor.com

It's all in how
you look at things.

Sunshine is delicious, rain is refreshing, wind braces up, snow is exhilarating; there is no such thing as bad weather, only different kinds of good weather.

anon@youaretheauthor.com

Fear less, hope more;
whine less, breathe more;
talk less, say more;
hate less, love more;
and all good things
are yours.

It pays to be nice.

Being nice doesn't mean drawing
the short straw all the time. Good
actions come back to bless me.

anon@youaretheauthor.com

You get the best
out of others when
you give the best
of yourself.

anon@youaretheauthor.com

There is no
conversation more
boring than the
one where
everybody agrees.

When all men think alike, no one thinks very much.

He who angers you
conquers you.

He who establishes his argument by noise and command shows that his reason is weak.

mark_sitw@lycos.com

I don't have to attend every argument I'm invited to.

Silence is one of the hardest arguments to refute.

The purpose
of life is a life
of purpose.

anon@youaretheauthor.com

Work, play, play play, play, work, play, play play, play, work, play, play play, play, etc.

Remember what the money's for!

Don't let work
take over your life.

anon@youaretheauthor.com

Find out what you
don't do well,
then don't do it.

Eighty percent
of success is
showing up.

Hard work spotlights the
character of people:
some turn up their sleeves,
some turn up their noses,
and some don't turn up at all.

anon@youaretheauthor.com

A successful person
is one who can lay
a firm foundation
with the bricks
that others throw
at him.

The roots of true achievement lie in the will to become the best that you can become.

anon@youaretheauthor.com

No one soars too
high if he soars
with his own wings.

anon@youaretheauthor.com

He who knows himself
is enlightened.

Empty your mind and the right answer will come.

When I try too hard to think of an answer it will not come. I think the Buddhists do the same thing to achieve enlightenment – just focus on nothing.

anon@youaretheauthor.com

When they discover the centre
of the universe, a lot of people
will be disappointed
to discover they are not it.

mark_sitw@lycos.com

Real knowledge is to know the extent of one's ignorance.

anon@youaretheauthor.com

Imagination is more
important than knowledge.

Knowledge is limited.
Imagination encircles
the world.

anon@youaretheauthor.com

To imagine is
everything;
to know is
nothing at all.

anon@youaretheauthor.com

Reality can be
beaten with enough
imagination.

rog2llus@yahoo.com

If you can imagine it,
you can achieve it.
If you can dream it,
you can become it.

anon@youaretheauthor.com

Doubts are traitors and make us lose the good we might win by being afraid to try.

Don't expect things to
go right the first time.

anon@youaretheauthor.com

Even the best laid plans go awry.

Never be afraid to go for plan 'b' — or to reevaluate yourself.

anon@youaretheauthor.com

Everybody makes mistakes.

Mistakes are proof that you're trying.

When I look back on some
of the things I missed,
I am immeasurably thankful.

sam-o@hotmail.com

Hard times are inevitable,
but misery is optional.

anon@youaretheauthor.com

The problem is not
that there are
problems.

The problem is
thinking that
having problems
is a problem.

Challenges are what make life interesting; overcoming them is what makes life meaningful.

anon@youaretheauthor.com

The best way to escape from
a problem is to solve it.

To the man who only has a hammer in the toolkit, every problem looks like a nail.

You can only choose from the options in front of you.

Never waste time on wishful
thinking or on unrealistic desires.

sidn.hopper@hotmail.com

We can try to avoid
making choices
by doing nothing…

…but even that
is a decision.

Any change, even a change for the better, is always accompanied by setbacks.

There must be an easier way.

If you don't like
something, change it.

If you can't change
it, change your
attitude.

anon@youaretheauthor.com

You must be the change you wish to see in the world.

If we don't change,
we don't grow.

If we don't grow,
we aren't really
living.

anon@youaretheauthor.com

Only the wisest and the stupidest never change.

Do it now –
tomorrow never comes.

anon@youaretheauthor.com

Enjoy the process.

There are many things in life
where the doing, the process of
creating or developing something,
is actually more important and
more enjoyable than the end itself.

jimbob-82@hotmail.com

Your time is the greatest gift you can give someone.

anon@youaretheauthor.com

Enjoy the little things.

If I hurry through life, I miss out
on some of the best bits.

anon@youaretheauthor.com

What lies behind us and what lies before us are tiny matters compared to what lies within us.

anon@youaretheauthor.com

Everything happens to
everybody sooner or later
if there is time enough.

Until you value yourself,
you won't value
your time.

Until you value your
time, you will not do
anything with it.

anon@youaretheauthor.com

Focus on now.

If I start thinking too far ahead
then I forget to enjoy the now.

anon@youaretheauthor.com

True wisdom is to live
in the present, plan for the
future and profit from the past.

anon@youaretheauthor.com

Don't cry because it's over;
smile because it happened.

anon@youaretheauthor.com

Things often happen when
you least expect them.

anon@youaretheauthor.com

Take life as it comes.

anon@youaretheauthor.com